FREAKED OUT

The bewildered teacher's guide to digital learning

Simon Pridham

Independent Thinking Press

First published by
Independent Thinking Press
Crown Buildings, Bancyfelin, Carmarthen, Wales, SA33 5ND, UK
www.independentthinkingpress.com
Independent Thinking Press is an imprint of Crown House Publishing Ltd.

At the time of writing and publication the version of operating system available on iOS devices shown in this book was 7.1 therefore the screenshots (some
screenshots show version 6.1.3) and instructions are suitable for this version.

The apps shown in this book are accurate to the date of publication and screencasts shown in the book are linked by dynamic QR codes, i.e. the QR code stays
the same but the content it links to can be changed, so if any of the key apps change then the screencasts which explain them can be changed by us.

Apple usually release a new version of iOS every Autumn, since the last major update from iOS6 to iOS7 was a very major one which changed the whole look
and feel of the operating system we don't believe that there will be a major change this Autumn (2014). But you never know what Apple's plans are.

Trademarks: All terms mentioned in this book that are known to be trademarks or service marks have been appropriately capitalised. Crown House Publishing Ltd
cannot attest to the accuracy of this information. Use of a term in this book should not be regarded as affecting the validity of any trademark or service mark.

Independent Thinking Press has no responsibility for the persistence or accuracy of URLs for external or third-party websites referred to in
this publication, and does not guarantee that any content on such websites is, or will remain, accurate or appropriate.

British Library Cataloguing-in-Publication Data

A catalogue entry for this book is available from the British Library.

Print ISBN 978-178135105-5
ePub ISBN 978-178135218-2

Printed and bound in the UK by
Stephens & George, Dowlais, Merthyr Tydfil

3 9547 00398 6432

Contents

Welcome to the start of your digital journey

Well, here goes! You are probably reading this book for one of three reasons:

1. You're a head teacher who has read stories about how tablet technology, and iPads in particular, are being used in education all over the world and you want to see what all the fuss is about. Is this just another fad?

2. You're a teacher in a school where the senior management team has decided to invest in iPads and a technology-enhanced curriculum. You are petrified!

3. You're a head teacher, teacher or any other professional involved in education who has plucked up the courage to learn more about the use of technology in education because you have just realised your 3-year-old son, daughter, niece or nephew is able to navigate their way around a mobile device with relative ease, while you are reaching for a manual and your glasses. You need help!

Irrespective of what category you fall into, or even if you are a parent or grandparent who wants to know more, *Freaked Out* is here to help you. So, what's my background and how can I help?

 I'm Simon Pridham @Freaked_Out123. In 2010, the primary school of which I was the head teacher gained seven grade 1s in an Estyn inspection. Following on from this, several sector-leading examples of practice at the school were highlighted by Estyn (Ofsted equivalent in Wales) and the Welsh Assembly Government. Everyone connected with the school was rightly proud and we felt our fantastic hard work as a school team had paid off.

Shortly after, I reflected on the previous twelve months (which had been hectic, to say the least) and challenged myself to take the school to the next level. But how? How was I going to lead my team forward and what was the vehicle for change going to be? I turned to a focus group of pupils and talked to them about their lifestyles, interests, preferred ways of learning and so on. The conversations I had with those children changed the strategic direction of the school forever and led me to ask myself an even bigger question: what is the role of schools and education in the 21st century?

After my discussions with that group of 11-year-old pupils something became very clear, very quickly. These pupils – using technology, peer support, networks of collaboration and mobile online resources – were able to build an education for themselves anywhere and at any time. A decade ago, information for your average 11-year-old was scarce outside the classroom walls. In 2014, information can be found in abundance. Google, YouTube, online blogs, social media, the list goes on and on but don't worry, we'll talk about this later.

Children no longer need to see their teachers as the font of all knowledge. In fact, they know they are not. Instead, they need to see their teachers as modellers of learning, master learners, risk-takers, facilitators, collaborators, creators and, to top it all, those teachers have to be tech-savvy. In today's child's world, content, knowledge and teachers are everywhere and accessible at all times. As educators, we have to change, and we should be excited about embracing the challenge and reaping the rewards.

So how do you do it? You need to have a love of learning, be able to model effective learning systems, be brave enough to take risks, be innovative and, most importantly, become a teacher of learning rather than a teacher of content, curriculum and facts. The 21st-century classroom, where technology is as accessible as pen and paper, allows you to personalise learning like never before, it allows you to develop independent and creative thinkers and it allows your pupils to drive their educational journey as co-pilots rather than passengers.

The days of constructing four walls with a podium at the front and calling it a classroom are over. Children are highly connected and consume information when and where it is needed. Developments like augmented reality (see Chapter 3) will certainly change the face of education as we know it – and already has in some cases. Successful classrooms now facilitate networking, small group collaboration and inter-action with the subject of study in a highly connected environment.

Before we get stuck into the nitty-gritty and you start your journey in earnest, I would like to give you an insight into how things have changed using my 3-year-old daughter as an example. My daughter has been born into a world where technology and, in particular, mobile technology is no big deal. From birth, she has been exposed to mobile devices, gadgets and computers and to vocabulary like email, blogging, websites, Wi-Fi and so on.

To her grandparents, this was alien talk a year ago, so I have invested time and effort in helping them to become connected and in tune to learning through the use of technology. But even now, at 3, my daughter is far more confident than her grandparents. This is the world in which she comfortably exists. She is not afraid to push buttons, to explore technology, to make mistakes and to start again, thereby developing self-confidence and becoming resilient and resourceful. This is not part of the mindset of many adults who passed through an education system which did not promote or even understand the importance of these key qualities.

A little while ago, when my daughter wanted to make a paper aeroplane, she handed me my tablet device and asked me for help. Her instinct was such that she knew what to do when she didn't know what to do. I'm not for one minute suggesting that she knew where to look online or whose blog to read, but she certainly had the wherewithal to realise that the tablet would connect us to something which could teach us. We ventured straight to YouTube where we had several videos to choose from on the first page of results, and she soon found one she liked the look of. Within minutes we knew what materials we needed to collect and she was pressing pause on the video. We built the aeroplane together step by step. I taught her how to rewind and play the video as we progressed, and an hour or so later we were testing her prototypes outside. We even took photos to show her grandmother and she asked if we could email them when we had finished playing in the garden.

Welcome to the world of learning in the 21st century! Pupils now learn from peers, online communities and experts who share their knowledge through traditional and online sources. As teachers and coaches of learning, we have a duty to provide the environment and opportunities that young people need to flourish. I think it is simply unacceptable not to be inspiring, engaging and enthusing pupils in this way.

Pupils aged 11–14 now have access to more information through their smartphones than I did in my entire university library as a student. Yet a high percentage of secondary educators still ban pupils from using smartphones in their classrooms. Talk about missing a trick, alienating a generation and turning pupils off school! What society needs are individuals who can ask good questions, come up with imaginative solutions, critically examine those possibilities, work out which creative solution is most likely to be effective and communicate it effectively enough to motivate others to action. The wise old owl, Albert Einstein, said, 'education is not the learning of many facts but the training of the mind to think'.

In short, the 21st century classroom should be flexible, creative and highly connective. Moveable, comfortable furniture is important to encourage small group collaboration and communication. We need tables and walls on which we can write freely and collate our thoughts and actions – learning walls. Each pupil should be placed in a skills bank and should be comfortable and at ease sharing skills and learning with peers, thereby making learning more equitable, with each individual contributing to the development of the whole class. There is no need to have a front or back to the classroom, or a teacher's desk or even pupils' desks.

Why do we allow the same group of pupils to sit next to each other in the same seats for a whole academic year and then wonder why they aren't engaged in their learning? Would you really want to sit next to the same person for almost ten months at a time and not have the opportunity to get out of your seat to ask your friend at the other end of the room for help? No, I thought not. Thriving learning institutions have classrooms that embrace the social, physical and emotional aspects of learning.

We must always remember that technology is simply one part of this effective learning environment. A creative curriculum, highly effective pedagogy and mobile technology *together* create the surroundings where pupils feel valued, challenged and effective. The days of the teacher being the purveyor of all knowledge at the front of the class are dead. Some of the best teachers my daughter will ever experience will be virtual, online and sitting on the other side of the world.

There is currently a debate brewing in technology-rich schools regarding accountability – to parents, system leaders, local authorities and our friends from inspectorate services and government. The debate goes something along the lines of: should we balance school life between using technology and more traditional methods such as writing with pens? And it's all about a balance between the two.

Until our assessment systems are radically overhauled, we are still going to need to prepare pupils for the end-of-year exam – using technology or not. But this doesn't mean I agree with it. Indeed, we should keep challenging the status quo, demonstrating that a technology-rich curriculum coupled with excellent teachers and industry engagement will ultimately raise standards, increase engagement, empower pupils, improve teachers and will scaffold the skills the next generation are going to need when entering the workforce.

We must be innovative and create systems that provide parents with the confidence that the effective use of technology is a must in their child's schooling. This will inevitably mean that school classrooms, school books, homework and the way pedagogy is delivered will be different from their own schooling. Society has evolved, people have evolved and the skills that employers now demand have changed dramatically. As schools and educators, we have an incredibly important duty to evolve at the same pace. If we don't then we are failing a generation.

For these reasons it is vital that the school's vision and purpose when using technology across the curriculum is communicated clearly to parents and community members, as well as system leaders, the inspectorate and local authority officials. Learning should be about choosing the right tool to solve the right problem. If we can instil these skills in children during primary school then they will leave us as independent, personalised learners.

I'm sure your mind is now racing with positive and inquisitive thoughts. How do you create a classroom where technology is as accessible as pen and paper? An environment where pupils have personalised learning experiences and are co-pilots in their learning journey? Well, it's all down to small steps, so let's take our first one together and meet your iPad.

Please note: Throughout the book you will notice that important words and terms are **highlighted**, these words are explained in 'A useful glossary' on p. 119.

Key to QR codes

 Information   Download

 Video

Chapter 1

Meet your iPad

The iPad is an intergenerational digital pencil case. By this I mean, if you lined up a 6-month-old child, a 6-year-old, a 16-year-old and a 66-year-old and passed the device along the line, each of them would find a functional use for it immediately. For you, as an educator, the ecosystem behind the device is second to none. So, what's all the fuss about and what does it do?

First, I'm going to take you through the basic functions of the iPad interface. It is important to know your way around in order to ensure maximum functionality and efficiency when your digital apprenticeship really begins. Let's get cracking!

Sleep/wake button

This does what it says on the box – the button turns the iPad on and off. Personally, I never turn my iPad off in this way as simply closing the case sends it into snooze mode – when you reopen the case you are ready to go again. However, if you do want to shut down you need to unlock the iPad, press the sleep/wake button or home button, drag the slider that appears on screen and close down. To turn it back on, hold down the sleep/wake button until the Apple logo appears on the screen. If you don't touch the screen for two minutes, the iPad will lock itself until you unlock it.

Sleep/wake button •———

Home button

The home button does many things, but its main function is to take you back to the home screen at any time. While there you can tap on any application to open it.

Siri

The home button allows you to access Siri, which is a very clever Apple tool that enables you to ask your device a question and it will do its very best to answer you. However, it is only available if you are using a third generation iPad or later. It is important to note you will need internet access and 3G or 4G coverage. To access Siri, you'll need to let your iPad know that you want to ask a question. Similar to the iPhone, you can do this by holding down the home button for a few seconds.

When activated, Siri will beep at you and a window will open on the screen containing a small microphone icon. The microphone will glow purple to indicate that Siri is listening. Simply ask a question and Siri will do its best to comply. If you want to ask additional questions while the Siri menu is open, simply tap the microphone. It will glow purple again which means you can ask away. Remember, a purple-glowing microphone means Siri is ready for your question, and a microphone that isn't glowing means he is not listening.

Side switch and volume

The side switch button allows you to silence any audio alerts or notifications. You can also set it to prevent your iPad from switching between portrait and landscape orientation.

The volume button does what it says on the box: controls volume manually on your device.

Side switch
Volume

Front-facing iPad and functions

Status bar

Apps

Home button

FaceTime camera

Multi-Touch

FaceTime camera

The FaceTime camera is a very useful tool and allows you to connect to another iPad, iPhone or Mac via video. I have used this extensively, both for continuing professional development (CPD) purposes by connecting with other educators around the world and for connecting groups of pupils to other schools and groups to develop national as well as international learning links. A great tool!

Multi-Touch display

One of the main advantages of using the iPad in schools is how simple it is to use. To use the iPad and its apps, just use your fingers to tap, drag, swipe or pinch/stretch.

App icons

There are many thousands of apps available in the App Store and we will be exploring the key ones to get you going and to develop you as a digital teacher later in Chapters 2 and 3. All the apps that come with the iPad, as well as any you download from the App Store, will appear on the home screen.

When you have opened an app, you can press the home button at any time to return to the home screen. Obviously, you can also swipe left or right to see other screens which have apps available to open. Another tick in the box for using the iPad in education is that it lets you run many apps simultaneously. If you need to view what apps are running at any one time, simply double-click the home button to reveal the multitasking display and swipe left or right to see more. To switch to another app, simply tap it.

Status bar

The icons in the status bar at the top of the screen provide information such as Wi-Fi status, the time and battery life.

Other features

The iSight camera is situated to the back of the device in the top-left corner, the speaker is in the bottom-left corner, the microphone is at the top in the middle and the headset port is top-left.

As you get to grips with your iPad you will discover many of these features for yourself but don't worry about this, most features are intuitive.

Chapter 2

What is an app and how do I get one?

I can remember first hearing the term 'app' early in 2011 and not having a clue what one was. Fast forward a few years and I can't imagine a day going by when I don't use apps, talk about apps, have an idea about making an app or when I'm not working with pupils or teachers and teaching them about useful apps.

Recently, I delivered a keynote speech to a group of local authority directors and councillors who were embarking on a digital journey and I used the word app in my introductory remarks. Afterwards, an official approached me and said, 'I enjoyed your talk immensely … but please can you explain what exactly an app is and what it does.' At first I felt a little deflated, as it seemed that the woman in question, who was delightful, hadn't listened or understood my message. However, as I reflected on her question it dawned on me that she simply wanted to understand how an app worked, what it was and why it was relevant to learners. This got me thinking and led me to carry out some research to gain a better understanding of where the app originated and also some current facts and figures regarding their impact.

The American Dialect Society named app the Word of the Year for 2010. This signifies that a term is trendy and growing in popularity; that recognition alone says a lot about the rise of the app. App is an abbreviation for application and taken literally it means: 'A self-contained program or piece of software designed to fulfil a particular purpose; an application, especially as downloaded by a user to a mobile device' (*Oxford English Dictionary*). Essentially, an application (or app) is a software application designed to run on smartphones, tablet computers and other mobile devices.

Where do you get one?

Apps are available through different app distribution platforms, such as the Apple App Store, Google Play, Windows Phone Store or BlackBerry App World. We will be concentrating on the Apple App Store in this book and like all app stores, some apps are free, while others are paid for. However, cost is something you must consider carefully as a teacher or head teacher, especially if you plan to roll out a one-to-one mobile device programme where every child in a class, year group, department or whole school has their own iPad for individual use.

What were apps originally for?

Mobile apps were originally offered for general productivity and information purposes, such as email, calendar, contacts, stock market and weather information. However, as innovators and educators collaborated, education apps soon followed, which have since led to teaching and learning being delivered in classrooms around the world in a way which was simply impossible in the past. It has also empowered the students, personalising their learning opportunities and giving them autonomy, again in ways which were not possible previously.

I don't think it's too big a statement to make that we have witnessed a digital revolution in education during the 2010s. Educators across the world need to sit up and take notice. Policy-makers should be thinking about the importance of these skills in our society today. Remember, we are equipping pupils for jobs which currently don't exist. Education can no longer be a parallel universe to society.

Creating an Apple ID and iCloud account

In this guide, I'm going to assume that you want to create a new email address for use with your Apple ID, so first I'll take you through the steps to create a free iCloud account and Apple ID.

There are five key steps involved in setting up an iCloud account:

Step 1

Tap on the icon opposite, which you will find on your home screen. This takes you to Setings. Now select iCloud.

To get a free **Apple ID**, insert your birth date when asked, and press **Next**. Insert your first and last name, and press **Next**.

Step 2

Now you can create your new free iCloud email address. Press **Create** and type in your password (it should be at least eight characters long and include a number, upper case and lower case letter).

Step 3

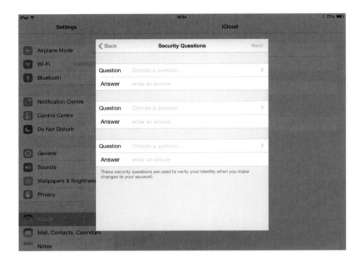

Next, choose and create answers for three security questions that you will remember. I recommend that you take a screen shot of your questions and answers once you are ready (press the home and power button at the same time to do this). This will allow you to keep them as a photograph for future reference.

The next screen will ask you for a rescue (alternative) email address which can be used to confirm your identity or reset your password. You will then be asked whether or not you want email updates from Apple. This is basically marketing material from Apple so it's not essential – it's entirely your call.

Step 4

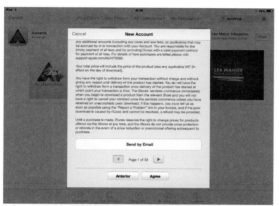

If you wish to read all the terms and conditions feel free. Alternatively, you can choose to press the **Send by email** button to peruse at your leisure.

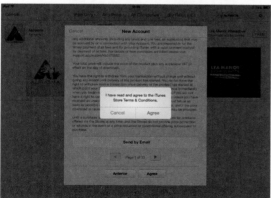

To continue to the next stage, press **Agree**, and then press **Agree** again when faced with the screen opposite.

Step 5

Your **iCloud** account has now been created and you will be faced with this screen.

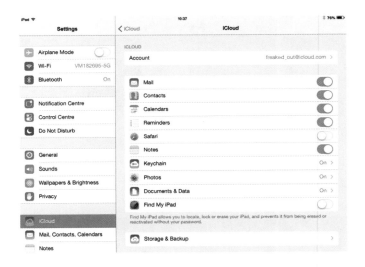

Note: Keychain is Apple's password management system and securely stores and encrypts your passwords. It is optional, but if you choose this you will need to input your mobile number for additional security.

Getting an app

You now have an iCloud account, so it's time to create an Apple ID to enable you to start down-loading apps.

Step 1

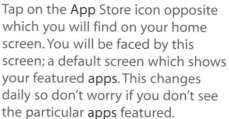

Tap on the **App** Store icon opposite which you will find on your home screen. You will be faced by this screen; a default screen which shows your featured **apps**. This changes daily so don't worry if you don't see the particular **apps** featured.

Look to the top right corner where you will find a search box. We are now going to download our first **app** together. Type in 'Aurasma' which is an **app** you will need in Chapter 3.

Your search should direct you to a screen which looks a little like this.

Aurasma is one of many free apps that you can download, whereas others have to be purchased. Please check carefully at this stage.

What is an app and how do I get one?

Step 2

Tap on Free to start downloading the **app.**

When Free changes to Install, tap on it and a **Sign In** box will appear.

Step 3

I know you think you don't currently possess an Apple ID, but this is where you will have to stick with me as you sort of *do*! Tap on the **Use Existing Apple ID** button which will enable your iCloud account in the store. Once in the App Store, you have to agree to Apple's terms and conditions before you can use your Apple ID. Bear with me, this will make sense.

Step 4

Now enter your iCloud details to activate your Apple ID and to download/purchase apps in the store.

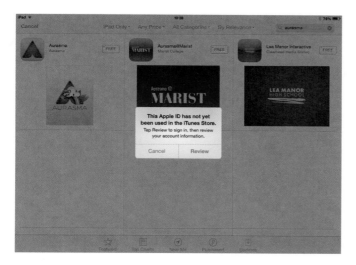

Once you've entered your details, press **OK** and you will be faced with this screen.

Tap on **Review** and it will ask you to confirm your location in the world (e.g. UK). Next will be the terms and conditions page which I suggest you agree to.

Step 5

Press **Agree** on the next screen which will lead you to the Billing Information screen.

Here you have some options:

1. You can register a credit/debit card, in which case you will be billed directly for any purchases you make in the App Store.

2. You can redeem an iTunes gift card.

3. You can choose to create an account with no payment options at all. This means you can do either of the above at a later date.

Step 6

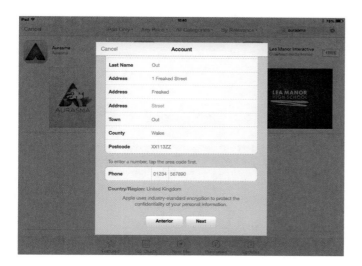

Fill in the personal details this screen asks you for. You're now good to go with your **Apple ID**.

Downloading the Aurasma app

You will see from this screenshot that the final stage of downloading the **app** is to enter your password.

The **app** will then download and will appear on your device.

Congratulations, you have now downloaded your first ever app!

Chapter 3
Where do I start and what do I do?

Now you have the fabulous Aurasma app, I'll show you how to follow the Freaked Out channel to make this book really come alive and how you can use this in the classroom.

Aurasma is an augmented reality app which allows you to bring 2D images alive by using them as triggers to activate video content or 3D images. So, how do you do that? Let's take a look together.

Step 1

When you open **Aurasma** for the first time, you will see this screen and message. Select **OK** and move on to the next stage.

Steps 2, 3, 4 and 5

These steps are short tutorials informing you more about what Aurasma can do. This way of working, by using augmented reality in the classroom as well as the whole school environment, is changing the face of education in digitally literate schools across the world. This book will now be transformed as you start to follow the Freaked Out channel.

To move through these screens simply flick the screen horizontally.

Step 6

You can now create your own account (which you can also do later) or you can simply log in if you already have an account. For the purpose of this chapter, I suggest you **Skip** and move on.

Step 7

Select the **A** at the bottom of the screen and you will be faced with the screen below right.

Step 8

You now need to search for the 'Freaked Out channel'. Tap on the **Search** icon.

Then tap inside the search bar to get the keyboard and type **Freakedout** into the search bar. Press **search** and away we go!

Step 9

You will be presented with a screen showing all of the search results.

Step 10

In the channel menu, select the option called 'Freaked Out' and you'll see this screen.

Step 11

Next press **Follow** and a tick will appear on the screen. We can now get interactive and accelerate your learning journey both professionally and personally.

Scan the image of the book cover below by selecting the ⌐¬ option at the bottom of the screen and holding your device over this page so that the picture is centred in the ⌐¬.

You might have to hold it steady and wait until the swirly image kicks in and the Aurasma film activates. By tapping the screen twice you will be able to move away from the image and watch the film on your device through the app. The only slight issue with the Aurasma app is that, because it compresses film so that it opens the trigger quickly, the quality isn't as clear as if you were accessing a YouTube channel. By tapping the screen once, it will take you to the Freaked

Out YouTube channel where you will see the difference in quality. If you move your iPad away from the book the film will stop.

In this book an image inside these markings ⌈ ⌉ indicates that you can use Aurasma to access more content.

Using Aurasma

Aurasma has the potential to be transformational both in the classroom and across the whole school environment. Think of the hundreds of amazing uses this app and augmented reality could have even if you just have one iPad in your classroom. Augmented reality is changing the way we educate, disseminate information and bring display boards and posters to life – the list goes on. So, what exactly is augmented reality and how can you use it effectively?

The concept of augmented reality has been around for some time now, but with the latest innovations in the digital world it has made huge surges in both education and learning contexts and has massive potential for school environments and community learning. Augmented reality is exactly what the name implies: an augmented version of reality which is created by mixing technology with the known world. In its most basic form, it is a simulation or, rather, a way of superimposing digital content into a real context.

For example, think of your classroom as a learning space. Consider the amount of information you display visually – the pupils' work, educational tips and prompts, generic inspirational material and so on. What each and every one of these displays asks a child or learner to do is to read them. We all know that everybody enjoys learning in a different way, so are we limiting the potential of our classrooms by just appealing to the readers when it comes to the learning space? In my experience, we certainly are.

I have worked with many schools and part of my job has been to advise teachers and head teachers on enhancing their learning spaces effectively by using technology. I think the answers pupils give when you actually stop and ask them what they would like to see on the walls, how they would like to interact with it and how much information they can absorb would surprise you. Ask your pupils and see what they say. Augmented reality offers the opportunity for peer modelling, effective feedback, engagement and, an essential ingredient in any successful class-room or school, amusement.

The origins of augmented reality go back to virtual reality in the 1950s. The most significant advances have occurred from the mid-1990s when researcher Tom Caudell coined the term 'augmented reality'. Some people confuse virtual reality with augmented reality, but there is a clear dividing line between the two concepts. In virtual reality you only experience and see virtual things. In augmented reality you're still seeing the real world, it's just that it has been augmented with some virtual information. It gives you actual information but it doesn't replace the real world you're experiencing.

A decade or two ago, augmented reality was exclusively used on computers through specific applications that users installed on their desktops. The introduction of mobile gadgetry, particularly smartphones and tablets, prompted app developers to design augmented reality apps that work best on mobile devices, hence the entry of augmented reality into the mobile era.

In a nutshell, augmented reality is about enhancing the real world by using digitised content. When you use a mobile application, the camera identifies and interprets a marker. The software analyses the marker and creates a virtual image overlay on the screen of the device, tied to the position of the camera. This means the app works with the camera to interpret angles and the distance of the mobile device from the marker.

A straightforward example is foreign travel. Imagine arriving in Paris and deciding you would like to do a sightseeing tour to discover the wonders of the city. Before the introduction of augmented reality apps you would have had to either buy a tourist guide or hire a tour guide. With an augmented reality app on your smartphone you can browse Paris and delve into its historical monuments the way you want. For example, if you hold your phone camera in front of the Eiffel Tower, it will both show you the real tower (reality) and will also provide you with nuggets of information on its history which will augment your understanding of that landmark (augmented reality).

By now I bet your mind is racing as to the mind-blowing potential of using augmented reality effectively in your school or classroom! Here are the five top ways in which I have used Aurasma with pupils:

1. Book reviews. When pupils have finished reading a book they can film themselves on the iPad, talking about it in the style of a review show. You can either scaffold this for them or give them free rein to talk about the book honestly, in readiness for the next reader. You can create an aura (this is an image which links to the video) of the book cover, linking it to pupil feedback and saving it to your school account, and make the augmented reality experience public. The reviewed books can be placed in a specific area of the school library or class so that pupils know all titles in that learning space have been reviewed using augmented reality. The next potential reader is then able to scan the book cover (their device should be following the school account) and listen to the review before deciding whether or not to read the book. This is particularly engaging for boys – it

encourages them to read more as they are keen to film themselves when they have finished the book. See p. 47 for an example of a student's book review using Aurasma.

2. Bringing pieces of art alive. Pupils film themselves going through the process of producing a creative piece of learning. They then drop the footage into iMovie and make a short film before saving the movie to the Camera Roll. You can now use the finished piece of art as the aura which, when scanned, will play the film. One word of warning: the footage shouldn't be too long as the file size will be too big and the audience will lose interest waiting for it to load.

3. Community links. One great project I led involved inviting over-seventies from the local community to bring old photographs of the village into the school as part of a locality project. They were interviewed about the images and then, once the pupils were happy with what they needed to know, they provided each intergenerational learner with a scaffold script. They were then filmed talking about their chosen picture and the films were saved to the Camera Roll.

The pupils created a large display which consisted of their own research, QR (Quick Response) codes (which we will discuss later) linking to local historical websites and the images which, when scanned using Aurasma, played the film of the intergenerational learner talking passionately about a particular part of the village which was important to them. All the work was saved to the school Aurasma account and anybody who followed the account could access the footage.

This brought the community together with a true skillshare ethos. It developed links with school stakeholders and made the learning between the 7-year-old and the 70-year-old equitable. They both realised that they had unique skills to share and were both developing knowledge while working together.

4. Communicating with parents/carers. Augmented reality should not only be limited to the internal school environment. Some schools I have worked with have transformed their community links by using to their advantage the fact that a high percentage of parents and careers now have smartphones. Consider how many times a parent doesn't apparently receive a newsletter or, if they do, they don't read it. In some schools, a large proportion of the adult community struggles with basic literacy skills, so a newsletter, website or blog is often not the best way to engage and inform. There is also the added issue of some families not having Wi-Fi or computer hardware at home. However, nearly all of them will have a smartphone on which both augmented reality and QR codes can be used effectively. Some schools use their school badge as the aura and create a news update or message each week which they link to the badge. Other schools place different signs for each class in the yard and parents are sent a text message to tell them when the board is 'alive' with a new film. You can imagine the amount of possibilities here – unbelievable!

5. Engagement. Using augmented reality as part of the fabric of what you do as a teacher and organisation lends itself brilliantly to a unique culture being fostered at your school. How many times have you heard a parent or grandparent say that they haven't got a clue about technology but their 5-year-old child or grandchild is a digital genius? The truth is they're not a genius, so don't reach for the phone to call Mensa quite yet. Remember the point I made in the introduction when I talked about schools getting ready for the 21st century learner today because children are born into a world where technology pervades all we do? As part of their adaptation to society, children are able to pick up skills quickly and gain huge self-belief in using technology at the same time. This is a huge opportunity for schools because, if done well, you can bolster self-esteem, pupil–parent relationships and community engagement all at the same time.

Some of the best examples I've seen have been pupil–parent workshops where the pupils taught their parents about benefits and uses of augmented reality and how it helps them to learn. Guides were then produced in both electronic and paper format, teaching parents how to download an app and follow the school. This was further built on by holding pupil–parent technology sessions where the pupils led the learning with their family members in a structured environment. Showcase evenings then followed and the whole community was invited to see the finished products and both parents and pupils spoke passionately and enthusiastically about the programme. The cynics among your parents will quieten down, the conversations about learning at home will become more frequent as the pupils realise that their parents just might have a clue about what they are explaining when asked the question, 'What did you do in school today?' and you have your community engagement machine well-oiled and purring.

The last thing a school or teacher wants when they start their digital journey in earnest is to encounter a lack of understanding by members of the school community. If you're a senior leader, take time to craft your vision, explain the benefits internally and externally, draw on research, clearly show how things have improved and, most importantly, put the children in front of them to blow them away. Stress that this is a joint journey between pupils and staff and how wonderful it is for pupils to see positive adult role models, like their parents and teachers, willing to learn from them. Very powerful!

Many cynics roll out the old chestnut that using mobile devices will be detrimental to the physical reading of books. I would take issue with this opinion. Does it really matter whether a child (or adult) enjoys reading a physical book, an e-book on an iPad or Kindle, a comic or a magazine? Surely, the main point is that they are reading, they are enjoying it and they are developing their decoding skills and literary understanding.

Your second **app**

In order to illustrate this and to demonstrate the power of Aurasma, you can now find out about your second app. Scan the icon below using Aurasma.

So, as I say in the film, now please download **Red Laser** from the **App** Store so that you can make this book come alive even more. Select the **App** Store icon and you'll see this:

Because the **app** is an **iPhone app** you will need to select the **iPhone** option and you will be taken to the second screen above. Download **Red Laser** and let's get busy! **To use the scanner, open the app and tap the [llll] icon at the top right of the screen.**

So, how can the iPad and certain apps enhance the process of reading and reviewing a physical book in your digital environment? One simple and highly effective way, which is excellent for engaging disinterested boys, is to use the app you already have some experience in – Aurasma (see Chapter 3). Now try this for yourself. See how the students made an Enid Blyton book review come alive with **Aurasma** by using the **Red Laser** scanner on the bar code opposite.

Now, imagine having focus books linked to specific topics or authors highlighted in your class and using this method of review and interactivity. Or a display board full of book covers and all class members completing an oral review throughout the term, linking to Aurasma and then displaying that on the live book board. Wow!

Exactly the same principle can be applied to any piece of learning you are displaying in your classroom or school environment. Just remember that you will need Wi-Fi or 3G coverage to be able to use Aurasma effectively. As a head teacher, I challenged all staff members to have at least two interactive aspects on every display board in the school.

Here you can see QR codes being used to enhance a 3D display of the solar system. The link takes you to the class blog page where pupils present their research about particular planets.

These external codes take parents and community members to the head teacher's blog and the home page of the school website.

This example from a Year 3 class shows a QR code which you scan to automatically follow the class Aurasma account. You can scan each piece of art and hear and see the pupil describe the process they went through in constructing their final artwork.

In this picture, you can see a pupil using his device to scan QR codes and Aurasmas housed on a 3D hexagonal task-setter. Pupils scan these to see what daily tasks they have been set and to listen to the teacher giving instructions on key tasks to be completed that day or week.

As you can probably tell from this book, QR codes are a terrific way to aid pupil and teacher digital development. In Early Years departments, I have witnessed teachers making great use of QR codes for phonic hunts, sound games and picture trails. The code can link you to a URL or text and so can be used for almost anything in your school. One primary school teacher colour-coded a number of QR codes and once the pupils had finished their set tasks, they scanned a code according to their groupings. This took them to an enhancement task which was to complete part of the class website page. The tasks were changed regularly and were allocated to different areas of the curriculum. This type of activity helps to develop personalised learning, independent thinking and peer support.

Another way I have seen QR codes used to increase parental engagement is for each class in the school to link their class web or blog page to a code. These codes are then displayed on noticeboards or outside in the school yard. Parents can scan the codes to see exactly what has been going on in their child's class that week. As the blog/web page is updated weekly, parents get to see at a glance the activities and learning taking place. Simple, but very effective.

You can also generate a QR code through an app called Audioboo which is basically a sound recorder. You can record yourself giving instructions or feedback, playing music or practising pronunciation of a different language and include these on school displays, in your school environment, newsletters or in your pupils' books.

Now scan the QR code and then press play to hear and see how Audioboo linked to QR codes can be transformational in your class/school and community. Once you have crafted your recordings within the app, click on share and then open in Safari.

Once there it will give you many options, one of which is to convert into a QR code. Click on that button and save to your Camera Roll. From there you have the code as an image and you can insert wherever you need to or print off and place it where you want to. The only limits here exist within your own imagination and creativity.

One point to note here is that you can make up to 10 minutes of recordings for free.

  Scan here using Red Laser to download Audioboo.

Chapter 4

How to inspire, engage and enthuse

These might seem like straightforward ideas when you are planning activities as a successful and passionate practitioner, but ask yourself one question honestly: could you truly say that over a day, week, month or school year that 75% of what goes on in your classroom actually inspires, engages and enthuses both you and your pupils? If you have answered yes then take a break from reading at this point, make yourself a nice cup of tea and treat yourself to a celebratory HobNob as you are in the minority.

The current education system, in my opinion, doesn't explicitly promote attributes such as inspire, engage and enthuse. This is partly due to a highly risk-averse system which values accountability, testing and data over creativity, personalised learning and collaboration. The society we live in is crying out for multi-talented young people who are able to adapt to challenges, both practically and intellectually, and who can themselves inspire, engage and enthuse others around them. The opportunity to use technology and mobile devices effectively throughout a school certainly allows school leaders to take the three pillars to the next level.

Here are the top ten points you need to feel really comfortable with if the iPad is going to inspire, engage and enthuse the teaching and learning in your school:

1. Your wireless network needs to be functioning effectively. Leave no stone unturned, as a failing wireless network will severely hamper iPad use.

2. Set out clear behaviour guidelines and link them to school policy. Involve the pupils and your digital leaders in putting together a code of conduct. This can be shared with parents and used at home as well so that there is consistency. Consistent expectations when using iPads can also help to prevent the device from being a disruption.

3. Start slow. Use one or two apps/functions and allow the students to get used to the device and its functions. Remember, mistakes will be made and there will be issues to resolve. It's all part of what makes the journey an exciting one!

4. The iPad is just a device and without an informed educator it will be ineffective as a learning tool. Your role is the master learner, but don't be afraid to ask your pupils for advice as they will be comfortable with many apps, procedures and skills – and it will boost their self-esteem.

5. Don't expect an app to 'teach' a lesson. I get bombarded with educators asking if there is a good numeracy, geography or art app out there. This is to miss the point of the iPad in education. Apps are just another tool to enhance learning – you will still use other methods to deliver lessons. Some of the most effective and inspiring lessons I have witnessed were delivered by teachers using the basic functions of the iPad brilliantly along with generic apps such as Explain Everything (more about this later).

6. Consider how you are going to display learning in class. The simplest method would be to link Apple TV to a projector, but there are other programmes to link a desktop to the iPad. With Apple TV, any iPad can be mirrored to the projector as long as the user knows

the password. When students are made aware that their learning could be displayed to the class at any time, it has a dramatic impact on their focus and productivity.

7. Be prepared for things to change as you and your pupils progress – and have fun doing it. There are so many opportunities to personalise a lesson when pupils have a device in front of them. As long as the learning objective is kept in mind, the students can all be doing something different to get to the same aim or objective in that lesson. Always ask yourself two things when this happens: first, can you assess what they have learned? Second, have they clearly shown how they have tackled the task? If the answer to both of these is yes, then brilliant!

8. Feedback is important. Your pupils are co-pilots on this journey so their views and opinions are crucial. Share your new skills with colleagues, peers and parents and ask them for their reactions. Remind them that they are all integral to the development of iPad use in the classroom.

9. With your senior leadership team and head teacher, decide on your workflow option when the time is right. In other words how and where you are going to save and store the completed learning on the devices. Knowing where the completed learning is stored and where it can be accessed and backed up is very important for everybody concerned.

10. Chart your journey and your experiences. Social media avenues, such as Twitter, are brilliant. I would also suggest starting a blog and sharing this. So many people are willing to help or discuss iPad use, so it makes sense to make use of the free professional development that is out there.

Recommended Apps

  Sarah Reece, a highly successful deputy head teacher and outstanding teacher and e-learning manager, has trialled many apps in her role and is always willing to share her experiences. Scan the QR code to listen to Sarah's top 5 dont's.

Don't

- Purchase as many apps as you can
- Expect staff to run before they can walk
- Expect to do this without release time
- Try to do it all yourself
- Expect staff to manage new apps on their own

Sarah and I have picked our top apps to get you going and also to provide you with a core set to begin your journey for real. You will notice two QR codes alongside each app. If you scan the first of these you will be able to tune into the Freaked Out YouTube channel where you can access short videos showing you practical usage of the apps described and ideas and tips on their functionality and capabilities. The second QR code will take you directly to the App Store where you will be able to download the app.

Top **Apps** to get you going

Please note: At the time of publication, some of these apps were free but others cost between £1.99 and £6.99.

1. iFiles

iFiles is a great app for teachers and pupils. It is best described as a file manager for iOS with features like connectivity to many cloud services which allow you to share documents throughout your classroom via Bluetooth or Wi-Fi. If you are using cloud services such as Google Drive, Dropbox, SkyDrive or iCloud, then iFiles supports all these and much more.

The app allows you to send documents to pupils' devices with ease. If you have pupil digital leaders in your class, you can also use it to develop a hierarchy of digital roles. (There is more on this in Chapter 6.) Another notable feature of iFiles is that it allows you to open up a web browser within the app and download content from YouTube, saving it to your Camera Roll. This enables you to use the relevant media as a tool with your class or to highlight specific material you would like your class to access.

The app is fantastic for pupils as it allows them to share learning in order to peer assess and to share skills to develop a culture of digital collaboration. Electronic books, documents and learning can be exchanged effortlessly around the digital classroom.

Scan here using **Red Laser** to go directly to the **App** Store and download iFiles.

2. Morfo

  Morfo is a wonderful app which can quickly turn a photograph of your friend's face, or any other object, into a talking, dancing, three-dimensional character. Once you have captured your photograph you can make your friend, famous historical character, sporting legend or object speak in a funny voice, a stern manner or an engaging tone. You can also make them dance! It is a simple, fun and flexible app which can be used by teachers to present instructions, bring a historical figure to life and deliver famous speeches or convey a key message via a sporting legend – the list goes on. You can also modify any of the six ready-made characters. Use your imagination and then save screenshots to use creatively when teaching.

You will find that pupils come up with some brilliant and imaginative ways to use this app. For them, it is a fantastic way to develop oracy skills and convey a message through role play. It also gives the reluctant speakers in your class a character shield to hide behind until they have developed enough confidence to really embrace speaking freely in front of their peers. I have witnessed pupils becoming Gustav Holst, Winston Churchill, David Beckham, David Cameron and many more when using the app.

  Scan here using Red Laser to go directly to the App Store and download Morfo.

3. Book Creator

With Book Creator you can create electronic books which can be shared with pupils or from pupil to pupil. You can also integrate movies, text, sound-clips and images to support the comprehension of a text.

The app is fantastic for aiding differentiation in any classroom. For example, if you are using a class novel as a stimulus in your literacy teaching, you could take a photograph of a page (or pages) of the novel and then record yourself modelling how that particular text should be read. This would help pupils whose target is to develop intonation when reading. It also allows pupils to read along with the text, which is particularly good for those who need practice in developing their decoding skills. As a teacher, you can also use this app to create electronic standardisation and moderation portfolios of evidence. These can be multimodal and offer the opportunity to give a rounded picture of a child or class's assessment.

So, there are many ways in which this great app can be utilised by you as a teacher to enhance the teaching and learning in your classroom or school – I bet you are scribbling down many ideas already. But how about the pupils? If you are fortunate to be teaching in a one-to-one classroom environment, then Book Creator provides an opportunity for your pupils to create digital portfolios during the school year or to develop a multimodal revision booklet which they can refer back to when they need to check information or to revisit a particular strategy.

See the app as a digital toolbox which supports all genres of writing, oracy and reading. It affords amazing opportunities to pupils in both primary and secondary schools. Writing can be brought alive with movies by using a combination of apps such as 8mm HD, which allows you to film footage in the style of, for example, the 1920s or 1960s. These films can then be dropped into an electronic book to create a multimodal learning text.

I witnessed a wonderful example of how electronic books can act as an enhancement tool in a primary school setting. A small group of pupils wrote a play script together in readiness for the visit of a community member to talk to the class about the Second World War. The group filmed their interview with the intergenerational learner, using their prepared script as a scaffold, and then dropped the finished article into their Book Creator piece, thus enhancing both their writing and oracy. Book Creator allowed the pupils to easily integrate various forms of media into one finished product which could then be shared peer to peer or used as a central resource. These examples illustrate the mantra I am constantly promoting throughout this book, which is that pedagogy, curriculum and technology together are the recipe for success.

Sharing your books could not be easier either as you don't need high-speed Wi-Fi in your class or school.

Scan using Red Laser to go directly to the App Store and download Book Creator.

4. Keynote

Keynote is the iOS equivalent of a PowerPoint app but, in my opinion, it is far more effective and easy to use whether you are a teacher or pupil. Keynote isn't PowerPoint – and that is a good thing. However, because Keynote and PowerPoint are both intended for the same purpose there is a lot of overlap in terms of features, so if you've used PowerPoint or Keynote on a MacBook you shouldn't have any trouble getting used to Keynote for the iPad.

Keynote's user interface is simple and streamlined – for me, the simplicity of the app is one of its main attractions. You can add video, tables, charts and shapes directly into your presentation just by tapping the Insert button on the top-right and choosing what type of media you would like to add. This enables you to present information in a very interactive, fun and exciting way. For the pupils, it is a great way to summarise learning.

Keynote is yet another app that allows you and your pupils to make effective, highly interactive and wonderful presentations very quickly without the need to log on to a computer and be static while producing the learning. One idea would be to allow all pupils in your class to carry out one structured oracy presentation a term, with either a literacy or numeracy focus. This would develop their self-confidence and self-esteem while giving them the opportunity to develop their public speaking skills. Usability means that Keynote is the app of choice for the majority of pupils and its intuitive interface means that it doesn't take an age to put together a professional, high quality presentation.

Scan here using **Red Laser** to go directly to the **App** Store and download Keynote.

5. Screencasting

Screencasting apps allow you to promote an inclusive culture within your learning environ-ment. For example, you could pre-record an activity or strategy with differentiated support materials for children with additional learning needs and those more able and talented, which then frees you up to fully concentrate on specific groups for that task or session. For those learners who struggle to read instructions, it is a fantastic way to show clearly what is expected of them, what the aims and objectives are for that particular task and to create a clear reminder of how they can achieve those within the lesson.

My preferred Screencasting app is Explain Everything. Explain Everything enables students of any age to create, collaborate, communicate and consume content. It is essentially an app with a whiteboard screen that allows users to create audio and video, animate, write and draw objects, all while recording in real time. The end products can be pictures, videos or even template projects. It's brilliant because it allows users to annotate any object on the iPad with the touch of a finger. It makes it easy for children to capture their screen and share it with virtually anyone. The screen and finished videos can be mirrored to a projector using AirPlay.

As a teacher, you can use Explain Everything to record lessons, create demonstrations and export videos to your blog or website which can then support your classroom instruction. I have also seen videos that pupils have created used as a fantastic assessment tool and resource in the classroom. I have also witnessed children using Explain Everything very effectively to describe sub-activities in maths (e.g. to explain how to multiply) and to outline the structure of a good story.

Many of the functions that interactive whiteboard software provides can be found in Explain Everything at a fraction of the price, making it a simple and cost-effective solution and/or replacement for interactive whiteboards in your classroom. In my opinion, it is one of the most versatile apps to have in your toolkit, so if I were you I wouldn't be able to wait to get started with it. A brilliant app!

Scan here using Red Laser to go directly to the App Store and download Explain Everything.

App smashing

What exactly is app smashing (or apps mashing) when it's at home? Well, this used to be called multi-apping and it simply means putting together a combination of apps to enhance learning or produce a finished product.

For instance, imagine your pupils are undertaking a science experiment. They could use the basic note-taking facility on their iPad to collate their thought processes, plan their experiment and record their findings. Then, by using the camera tool on their device, they could take photographs at key points throughout the experiment. Next, they could drop their photographs into an app called Skitch which allows you to annotate pictures and add symbols such as arrows and speech bubbles. At this stage, the group could use their annotated pictures and notes to make a screencast using Explain Everything. Finally, they could then save it to Google Drive (for more information see p. 77) and share the screencast with the teacher or other pupils to show exactly what they learned before, during and after their experiment. This is a wonderful example of how pupils can use different apps to build a mini project quickly and effectively and before sharing their processes, thoughts and findings with others.

The skill of app smashing takes time to develop, both for you and your pupils. It will also take a lot of experimenting and playing around with your device before you become confident and multi-skilled in a number of apps (although I'm talking a few weeks rather than months). One of the huge benefits of mobile learning on the iPad is that it is easy to use and easy to pick up.

As well as these top apps, there are a few others that I would recommend as key components in your digital armoury when starting your journey. The excellent toolkit (on p. 65), designed by Pete Sanderson of @LessonToolbox, takes a great set of apps and splits them into designated areas which will allow you to experiment across the curriculum. I never like recommending apps for subject areas as for me it's missing the point. Remember, boring stuff on an iPad is still boring. However, these are all excellent apps and the fact that Pete has provided a brief description and highlighted key areas makes it very helpful.

When you are starting out there are two important tasks which you need to know how to do to move from the survival stage towards mastery:

1. Arranging your apps

Organising your device is important for teachers and students, so arrange your apps so they are in an order you are comfortable with and you know where to find them. To move them around, touch and hold any app on the home screen until it jiggles, then simply drag it around. When you have downloaded more than a handful of apps you will find that you want certain 'pages' of apps. To move apps from one page to another you need to drag the app to the edge of the screen or to the dock at the bottom of the screen. To save your changes just press the home button and it's job done.

2. Creating folders

I highly recommend that you organise your apps into folders (e.g. key apps, literacy, numeracy, note taking, photography, workflow). Simply drag one app on top of another which will then create a folder. To rename the folder, just tap the folder name. Drag apps to add or remove them from a folder. When you are happy with your new arrangement, press the home button.

@LessonToolbox's – Apps for Learning

Video Apps

 Vine (free) Create short (6 second), looping videos

 iMovies (installed) video making and editing, with movie trailer features

Blogging Apps

 Wordpress (free) –online text with embedded images, and links

 Blogger (free) – online text with embedded images, and links

 Glogster (free) – interactive posters which can include videos, text, web links etc

Video Blogging

 Touchcast (free) – Enhanced video that is fully browsable, responsive, and can include web pages, images, and videos inside the live stream

Interactive Pictures/Posters

 ThinkLink – Use ThinkLink to instantly add video and text to images

Podcasts

 Audioboo (free) –Record up to 3 minutes for free. Post your clips easily to the web

 Spreaker (free) – Create and share LIVE audio broadcasts on the go from your mobile device

 Soundcloud (free) – Record audio with one touch and easily share it to Facebook, Twitter, Google+ and Tumblr etc

 Voicethread (free) – Add images and videos from your camera or photolibrary. Flip through pages and annotate them while you narrate. Share by sending email

Sharing Ideas and Resources

 Evernote (free) – Create and edit text notes, to-dos and task lists
⏻ Save sync and share files
⏻ Record voice and audio notes
⏻ Search for text inside images

 Pintrest – Pin images from around the web. Explore pins and boards on different topics

 Twitter – Get real-time stories, pictures, videos, conversations, ideas, group discussions

 Edmondo – Secure classroom discussions, posting assignments

 Office 365 (subscribers only) – Secure classroom discussions, sharing resources

Animation

 PuppetPals/PuppetPals 2 (already installed on all iPads) that lets you create animated cartoons

 Tellagami (free) – create and share a quick animated video

 Shadow Puppet – Record a puppet and talk through your photos. Quickly and easily create a narrated slideshow to share your stories

In-Class Assessment

 Socrative - short answer questions, quick quiz, multiple choice, class voting (essential app!)

Mind Maps

 Popplet – installed – mindmapping software (VERY easy to use)

Picture/Video Enhancers

 Memegenerator –Makes memes (pictures with text)

 Quipio – Also make memes but with better quality finish – looks professional

 Coach's Eye –review video with slow-motion playback and drawing tools

Courtesy of Pete Sanderson
@LessonToolbox

Pedagogy, technology and a creative curriculum = possible magic!

When taking your first steps and embracing technology as a teacher it is important to remember that you are not alone. The teaching community is an extremely generous one and there are some outstanding practitioners and leaders out there who are willing to share their mistakes, highs, lows and experiences along the way.

I have learned so much from pioneers like Fraser Speirs, Andrew Jewell and Jenny Oakley from the wonderful Cedar School of Excellence in Greenock, Scotland. I also visited inspirational schools with a fantastic story to tell, like the Essa Academy in Bolton, where the charismatic Abdul Chohan helped to guide us on our school journey. I now class colleagues like Fraser, Andrew, Abdul and Jenny as friends, and I can guarantee you too will meet fellow professionals who will become good friends and colleagues who you will learn with and from for a long time.

Laura Poiner is a classic example of how sharing skills can be transformational to your career. Back in 2011, Laura left the school for a term's secondment to develop her skills in another area of the curriculum. In her absence the school embarked on their one-to-one mobile device programme. On her return it would have been easy for her to use this absence as an excuse to not understand or embrace the new philosophy of making technology as accessible as pen and paper to the students. Instead, however, she insisted on learning, experimenting, listening to her digital leaders and spending her own time asking questions and learning from the e-learning manager, Sarah Reece. As a result, she has become a key member of the school's middle management team, has increased her skillset dramatically, is a key delivery expert for digital CPD and has taken her career to a whole new level. Laura is a classic example of a teacher who has flown and has transformed her pedagogical delivery, environment and mindset.

  Scan the QR code opposite to listen to Laura's top five key improvements from using technology in the digital classroom.

1. Sharing worksheets, resources (iFiles see p. 57).

2. Create e-books for guided reading and teaching reading skills (Book Creator see p. 59).

3. Stating learning objectives and improving settings (Scroll 'n Roll see below).

4. Explaining homework (ShowMe – a similar app to this is Explain Everything, see p. 62).

5. Interactive display (Aurasma see p. 31).

Most of these apps we have mentioned previously but here's some information about Scroll 'n Roll:

Scroll 'n Roll

  Do you know those scrolling text messages which you typically see when there is breaking news on the television or the latest big name footballer has just signed another multimillion pound contract? Well you can use the Scroll 'n Roll app the same way in your classroom to set lesson objectives and aims, give feedback and communicate important messages and challenges throughout the day. A good, useful tool indeed!

One of the best ways to chart your journey is by starting a blog right at the beginning. WordPress is a great place to begin. I have listed some of the best blogs out there written by practitioners who are teaching every day. Reading their posts will help you to build up ideas and learn from other's mistakes, which I firmly believe will give you confidence.

Blogging is basically an online diary of information which can be accessed through the World Wide Web. Most of the world's leading digital educators have blogs and are only too willing to share their work, resources, tips and material.

My top recomended blogs

Scan the QR codes below to read some excellent blogs regarding digital journeys and how technology can enhance the teaching and learning process.

  Mark Anderson:
http://ictevangelist.com

 Sarah Reece and Mike Elliot:
http://ipadshare.wordpress.com

  Dan Edwards:
http://dedwards.me/

 Learning with iPads:
www.learningwithipads.co.uk

Chapter 5

What is the digital environment?

Think about this question carefully: do you want your school or classroom to be a parallel universe to what exists outside the school gates?

As you are reading this chapter, pupils around the world are accessing various forms of information as well as communicating on 3G and 4G networks. However, many secondary schools try to suppress the use of mobile phones in classrooms by confiscating them on arrival or simply banning them on school grounds. In my opinion, this is simply down to a lack of understanding by school leaders in realising how simple smartphone tools can transform the learning environment in an instant.

Here are some examples of basic functionality which I have seen used effectively in secondary schools across the UK:

● Calculator

● Voice recorder

● Timer

● QR code reader

● Foursquare (to help new pupils navigate around the school)

● Note-taking

● Twitter

● Virtual field trips

● Online calendars

These are simple but highly effective uses for mobile phones in the classroom, without even mentioning Wi-Fi, devices purchased or leased by the school, or teaching and learning. I understand the concern by secondary school colleagues regarding, for example, pupils posting inappropriate content on social media sites but the simple answer is to heavily involve the school digital leaders (see Chapter 6) in constructing a consistent code of conduct for all pupils. This has to be communicated forcefully and reinforced constantly through all channels to students and parents. Interactive posters throughout the school are a great way to get the message across as well as via more traditional means.

If this code of conduct is broken there is a sanction, in exactly the same way that there is a sanction if a pupil throws a chair across the classroom or has a disagreement with another pupil. Life in schools is quite straightforward in this respect: for every action there is a consequence – some good, some not so good.

This simple but very effective traffic lights system for secondary classrooms was made by the outstanding Ed Tech educator, Matthew Pullen, who is an Apple Distinguished Educator (ADE).

Let's get back to how you can use technology and an enhanced classroom environment to aid teaching and learning and promote that all-important mantra – engage, inspire and enthuse.

As a teacher or leader new to developing a digital environment, I think there are certain headings under which you can take a stepped approach, evaluating the impact along the way and sharing your experiences with other staff members in staff meetings and twilight sessions.

So far, we have looked at displays and, providing you have Wi-Fi in your school, this is a great way for everyone to start embracing technology by changing your display policy and making sure all school boards have at least one or two elements of interactivity. What else can you get cracking with in your classroom?

Projector and Apple TV

An Apple TV is a little confusing until you know exactly what it is. The first thing to understand is that it is not, as its name would suggest, a TV made by Apple. It is actually Apple's own media streamer, and it's pretty much as simple as that. Apple TVs can be purchased from any reputable high street electronics store, from Apple directly in store or online, or from any well known online stockists, such as Amazon.

A media streamer is a device that plugs into your TV or HD TV which allows you to watch films, movie trailers, TV shows, home videos, photos and other media from either computers or devices on your school or home network or directly from the internet. Whether you have one iPad just for yourself, a group set or are a one-to-one class/school, using Apple TV increases engagement, enables you to seamlessly mirror to your whiteboard from your device and allows your pupils to show their learning to the rest of the class for them to peer assess. Pupils can also use the camera and video facility in their device to stream content.

The six key benefits of using Apple TV in the classroom are:

1. The teacher can share iPad content from anywhere in the classroom on a high definition screen.

2. The pinch and zoom feature on the iPad makes for detailed viewing with diagrams, maps, images and reading selections.

3. Pupils and pupil groups can connect and present from any location in the classroom.

4. Live annotation on the iPad enables the teacher to move around the classroom and better monitor and interact with the pupils.

5. The camera can be used to project live shots of teacher and pupil experiments or learning to others in the room.

6. The iPad can be used as a visualiser, highlighting anything for all to see in the classroom.

Scan the image of the Apple TV to the right using the Aurasma app to see the power of Apple TV.

This time tap on the live video once and it will take you to a YouTube link. This will show you the slight difference in film quality when linking to YouTube. Consider this when planning your work with Aurasma.

Workflow and accountability

I like to use something called accountability slips because they help pupils to explain why they have chosen to use their iPad to complete a particular piece of learning, whether to enhance it or to use various apps to finish an open-ended task. For anybody scrutinising the pupils' books, they now have a workflow trail and the pupil's evaluation and explanation as to why they chose that route.

Obviously, this is not an option for every lesson but as the pupils enter the upper end of primary school, these opportunities for personalised expression within learning should become more frequent and should inform our assessment, as well as making technology as accessible as pen and paper for all our pupils.

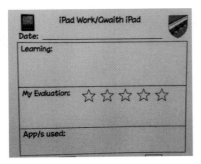

Here is a copy of the accountability slip. Please scan the QR code opposite the slip to see how it works and listen to a digital wizard explaining why they are so important.

Workflow and digital marking

One common question I am asked is, how do you mark learning on an iPad? Do you have to print everything off the device? Well, you'll be pleased to know that this is not the case. There is an app called Showbie which allows pupils to send you pieces of learning which you can then annotate and mark digitally on your own device. You can leave oral feedback and then return the work to the pupils when you are ready. Scan this QR code to the left to watch this in action.

Showbie

When your digital expertise progresses and you are asking pupils to send you learning to be electronically marked and returned to them, Showbie will become an essential app. It is the electronic equivalent of collecting in exercise books to mark.

Showbie allows you to assign, collect and review pupils' work. As a tool, it meets a demand that used to be supplied by the school VLE. The difference here is the ability to 'open in' a multitude of apps to create content or provide feedback. A couple of taps sees a piece of learning opened and annotated with audio feedback or viewed in the teacher's app of choice. It is then just as simple to return the piece of learning to the pupil for immediate viewing.

Showbie works very well with larger classes where the transfer of information is frequent. For secondary schools, it is very convenient as pupils can send the teacher work over a weekend, for example, and the teacher can leave feedback, return it and the student can amend the work before final hand-in on Monday. A great app!

So far we have looked at interactive displays throughout the school, seamless projection of learning within the classroom via Apple TV, addressed accountability and workflow. Now it is time for effective storage of digital learning and the creation of digital portfolios. For this I would highly recommend Google Drive.

Google Drive

Google Drive is fundamentally a cloud storage service. But what exactly does it do and how does it help your digital environment and that of your pupils and parents?

Google Drive lets you store and access your files anywhere – on the web, PC or Mac, on your iPad or any android device. So, straight away you can imagine the opportunities this brings for you and your pupils to start a piece of learning at home or school, save it in Google Drive, go home or back to school and open up the document, revise it, put it back on Google Drive and then reopen it at the next place you are going to be. It is an amazing digital toolbox for schools embracing a mobile roll-out programme or even if you have a class set of iPads which are shared across the school because more than one account can be accessed on a single device.

  Scan this QR code to watch how easy it is to save learning to a digital folder on an iPad using Google Drive.

Here's how it works. Sign up for a Google account (Gmail) on the web at drive.google.com. Install Google Drive on your computer or mobile device. Place your files in Google Drive from your device. Now your files go everywhere you do! Change a file on the web, on your computer or on your mobile device and it updates on every device where you've installed Google Drive.

Share, collaborate or work alone, your files are now extremely visible, portable and not device specific.

You are able to store the first 30 GB of your material for free across Google Drive, Gmail and Google+ Photos. This opens up a new world to you with regards to the digital environment as, in essence, it is now all around you and your pupils. Google Drive is part of the Google Apps suite which in itself is outstanding, but that's a conversation for another day.

As a school you can set this up through Google Apps for Education and, mark my words, it will be a brilliant development step for pupils, teachers and parents.

 Scan this QR code to take you to the website and to see the many benefits that registering your school will bring.

Structure

Schools which use Google Drive effectively across their organisation and community have similar set-ups to the one outlined below.

Every pupil has their own Gmail account which is protected so that pupils are only able to email internally to peers and staff and are unable to send mail externally. Likewise, no external mail can be sent to pupils directly.

Each pupil has a Numeracy, Literacy and Across Curriculum folder on their device (in Google Drive) so they can save their digital learning in the appropriate place once they have completed it. The beauty of this is that they can open that same piece of school work on any device at home and can share it with their parents, peers or grandparents, as long as they have the appropriate app installed. Imagine how easy it is to set homework in this way and receive it on a Sunday afternoon to edit via Google Drive and Showbie?

So, you can access everything in your Google Drive from all your devices. Your files are always waiting for you at drive.google.com, but you can also get them from your computer, smartphone or tablet. If you install Google Drive on multiple devices, the software makes sure they're all in sync. You can even get to your files when you are offline. Any time your device has internet access, it will check in with Google Drive to ensure that your files and folders are always up to date. Change something on one device and it changes everywhere. As a development step for all staff at your school, you could get them to stop emailing important attachments and start sharing them instead. Google Drive is fantastic for collaborative learning, peer assessment and developing great home–school links.

A big part of successfully integrating a mobile device programme into your school is to educate, coach and mentor not only the parents of your pupils but to use intergenerational learners in your community, such as grandparents. This is crucial to building strong relationships and fostering community cohesion. Forward-thinking schools have held Google Drive workshops, termly open learning sessions and after-school pupil–parent iPad courses. I cannot stress enough how important this is as you will need these guys on board from the outset so that you are not met with any misunderstandings about why you are embarking on this journey. Embracing a mobile tech digital programme is a unique opportunity to up-skill all community members, irrespective of age, ability or skill level. I have led very effective community cohesion programmes across the UK and tend to call them *skillshare projects*.

Skillshare projects

The way skillshare projects work is quite simple, but if done properly they can be highly effective in getting intergenerational learners into your schools to share with your pupils the more traditional skills that are often lost in the curriculum, while your pupils share their technology skills with the older generation.

How?

You have to start by asking the over-sixties, over-seventies and even the over-eighties in the community what skills they have and would like to use socially. From experience, the best way to do this is to put on a buffet in the school hall and then invite them in with their grandchildren as part of a community meeting. Free food is the way to get your community into the school in the first instance!

You will find that you have a broad range of individuals with a wide selection of skills. There may be highly skilled people with a wealth of life experience who are able to sing, sew, knit, own an allotment or there may be retired professionals with a background in banking, sport, teaching, nursing and many other areas.

Why?

I see this as a wonderful opportunity for older primary pupils to develop skills which are sometimes lost to the increasingly numeracy and literacy-focused curriculum. Used creatively, these skills can enhance and contribute to great numeracy and literacy teaching and learning. A creative curriculum, along with excellent teachers and schools, can take an 82-year-old grandmother who loves knitting and turn that experience into a sector-leading piece of work with pupils. Throw one-to-one iPad provision and a Wi-Fi network into the mix and, hey presto, things start to happen!

What happens?

From the initial community meeting, you might end up with around ten or more intergenerational learners, who will need to have a Disclosure and Barring Service (DSB) check before they become part of the school curriculum for a whole term. I have seen their skills integrated into teaching and learning themes and as part of extra-curricular provision. For example:

- A gentleman who sang in the local choir gave up an hour a week and helped out with a teacher at an after-school choir club.

- A gentleman who ran the local allotments came into school on a weekly basis and helped run the eco/gardening provision with the eco schools coordinator and pupil group. He taught them all about planting, growing and harvesting fruit and vegetables. The produce was then used as an entrepreneurial tool to learn business skills.

- A retired banking professional helped with business plans linked to the above initiative.

- A group of 70 and 80-year-old grandmothers (who were affectionately known as the Knitting Crew) came in to speak to a group of 9 to 11-year-olds and taught the pupils how to sew and knit while they were studying the Second World War and the 'make do and mend' ethos. This work inspired instructional writing, role play and other literacy activities.

Pupil digital payback

Once you have built up a hierarchy of pupil digital leaders in each older primary class (see Chapter 6), part of their role will be to work closely with community members. This is an important strategic move as you must integrate and educate parents and the community into the vision and developing digital culture of the school.

So, your digital leaders will work with the intergenerational learners you have recruited to teach them how to enhance their lives by learning new digital skills. It is advisable to hold a number of workshops beforehand with your digital leaders to give them taster sessions. Then you are ready to go. For example:

- The digital leaders, under the direction of the e-learning manager, taught the chorister how to Skype with his relatives in Australia (he had heard of Skype but didn't know how to use it).

- The gentleman from the allotment learned how to blog about his skills and the pupils even helped him to set up a website. He now shares his expertise and tips online.

● The Knitting Crew were taught how to shop online at the local supermarket, as they found this an arduous task during the winter months.

Brilliant! All of a sudden, the 7-year-old and 70-year-old start to cross the road to talk to each other about learning. I have led similar projects in other schools and communities with a similar impact. This is a fantastic way to involve your community, alongside pupil–parent technology sessions, once pupils and teachers have built up their expertise.

Chapter 6

Who are the digital leaders?

This chapter could easily have come right at the beginning of this book as, without a doubt, I see the role of the pupil digital leader as vital in a successful school mobile device programme. Think back to the introduction where I described why we must embrace technology in education and how our youngest pupils are being brought up in a world where technology is pervasive, where they've adapted to their technology-rich surroundings from birth and are entering our nursery schools with digital skills and vocabulary.

It would be a misconception to suppose that we now have a generation of 5-year-old digital geniuses. We don't. We have pupils who are able to turn on an iPad, navigate their way around the device and access apps and tools, but at that age they cannot create content and don't have the necessary skillset to effectively use the device to dramatically aid their learning.

However, the majority of 10 and 11-year-olds do have the required knowledge because they have been using iPads productively for three or four years. The secret is to use their skills correctly, highlight them in a digital leader programme and use them as co-pilots on the school's digital journey. But how do you identify them? And what exactly is their role?

How do you identify digital leaders?

My role working for the Welsh Assembly Government, as their Learning in Digital Wales professional adviser, was to look at effective digital leader models across the country and further afield and to highlight best practice, to produce case studies and to find key components which were consistent in the successful implementation of these programmes.

The identification process varies from school to school and from year group to year group. At the last school where I was the head teacher, for example, we began a media club at lunchtime and after school and built up expertise linked to the school's teaching and learning aims in a core group of pupils using technology as an enabler. This group of pupils from 9 to 11-year-olds quickly became experts in using mobile devices and key applications to enhance their learning.

We concentrated on the new Apple equipment we had procured in 2011 and our digital leader model was built around this hardware. We realised almost immediately that pupils' confidence levels in using the equipment was incredible and far surpassed the adaptability of the majority of teachers! Our digital leader model has evolved dramatically over the last few years and our identification and application processes have developed too.

During the summer term, the outgoing 11-year-old digital wizards from Year 6 run a two-week programme where they advertise the posts of digital wizard and digital leader in amongst their younger peers. The wizards are highly skilled digital champions who teach other pupils, staff members, community members and so on, whereas the digital leaders are one rung below on the ladder in terms of their skill set. The 8-year-olds, who are new to one-to-one provision, first undergo a term of getting used to their new device which will accompany them on their learning journey. With the help of their teacher, e-learning manager and the older digital wizards, they decide together who will become wizards and leaders. The process of how children become a digital leader in upper primary school is outlined below.

The Digital Leader Process

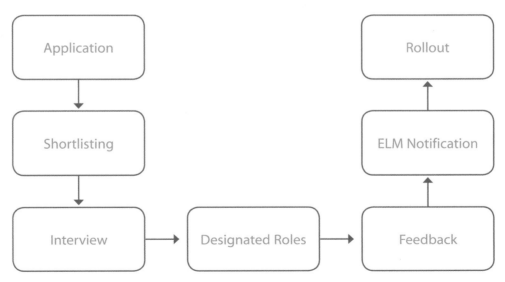

Source: Example from Casllwchwr School

Scan this QR code to watch a film about digital leaders.

Digital Leaders Hierarchical Structure

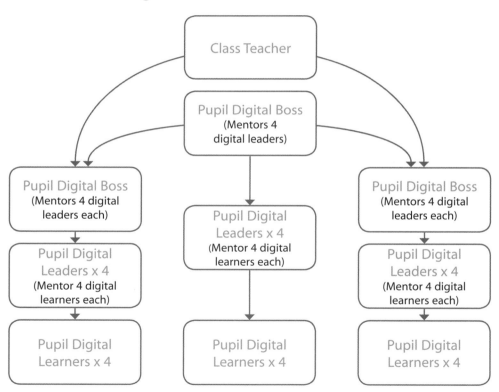

The digital leaders and the e-learning manager present the results to the teachers concerned during a staff meeting and issue them with a hierarchical structure of digital distributed leadership including all pupils involved, as in the example on p. 86. This process empowers your pupils and builds an effective peer assessment and mentoring model throughout your school. These skills are essential as we need our pupils to be able to think critically, to find solutions, to collaborate when learning and to be able to use technology to assist them.

In this class, the wizards selected three digital wizards and seven digital leaders, so the rest of the pupils have the opportunity to speak to a digital mentor on a daily basis. It might be that some of these pupils are very able digitally but choose not to become a wizard or leader. This is perfectly fine but, to you as a teacher, it should highlight that the child may need work on their self-esteem or confidence-building or some time spent with them explaining the importance of sharing their skills.

The majority of digital learners realise that they will need help sometimes and this system means they have a mentor available to help them when necessary. The digital wizards and leaders should be given badges to wear so that they are easily identifiable around the school campus. Pupils are allowed to move around the classroom to access help or information and, with the iPad being a mobile device, it can obviously accompany them. I have found that oracy skills and the articulation and evaluation of learning tools develop at a rapid rate as pupils spend time assisting each other and explaining. The beauty of this model is that it does not require you, as the teacher, to know everything about an iPad from day one.

Remember, I talked before about a digital journey together with your pupils, with co-pilots learning and assisting each other – well, this is it! What a unique and amazing opportunity for you to be seen as a true lifelong learner as part of this process. Amazing!

The e-learning manager and class teacher obviously need to spend time and expend effort with your digital wizards and leaders to ensure they develop their skills. Media clubs, genius camps, after-school clubs, lunchtime sessions and transition projects are all great vehicles to plan, implement and evaluate digital leader programmes in your school.

The role of digital wizards and leaders

Their main job description includes:

- Housekeeping – charging devices each night and looking after the general upkeep of hardware.
- Working closely with the e-learning manager and class teacher.
- Sharing skills with other pupils in class on a daily basis.
- Attending extra-curricular digital sessions to learn new skills.
- Representing the school at training days or conferences.
- Sharing skills with pupils from other schools.
- Taking i-assemblies with the e-learning manager.
- Producing a digital leader blog and weekly podcast.
- Producing screencasts and tutorials for teachers, pupils and teaching assistants.
- Testing new technologies and their impact on teaching and learning.
- Being involved in policy-making with the e-learning manager and senior leadership team.

- Making presentations to governing body and parents.
- Helping to run pupil–parent mobile device training.
- Helping out with intergenerational skillshare programmes.

  When starting out, keep it simple and begin in one class so that you can evaluate the impact and structures you may need. The system may need tweaking to get it right and, as I have stressed throughout this book, it takes time to implement new systems effectively. There is a huge amount of good practice out there – a great leaflet was distributed by Rising Stars at BETT (the British education, training and technology show) 2014 called 'Getting Started with Digital leaders: A Practical Guide' which you can access if you scan this QR code. This will give you additional information and detail when you are ready to develop your programme.

Deputy head teacher, Sheli Blackburn, does fantastic work with the Digital Leader Network, which is an organisation that you should certainly consider joining when you feel the time is right to find out about new ideas and resources, to collaborate and to showcase your pupils' work.

 This QR code will take you directly to the Digital Leader Network site: www.digitalleadernetwork.co.uk.

Start your digital leader programme in the first week of your personal journey as it will give you support structures, expertise, confidence, self-belief and will change the learning culture in your classroom for the better. Over time you may well develop distinct groups of digital leaders throughout your class and school. Some may be especially skilled in computing, programming, digital literacy, e-safety, iPads, app development or other areas. You will know when the time is right to add on these extra layers and make the model fit for your school. Remember, we are all co-pilots on a digital journey together.

Good luck!

Chapter 7

What about security and control?

A whole book could be written on security and control for school mobile device programmes, but in this chapter I will cover the essentials that you will need in your school and which can then be shared with colleagues and the e-learning manager to implement across the school.

An important point to consider when rolling out mobile devices across a school or scaling up your digital provision is technical support. You may be extremely fortunate and have an excellent support team within your local authority who can provide this service. However, this is often not the case and so you will need either a technician within the school, if you are secondary school, or it might be possible for a primary school to share a technician with a catchment secondary school.

There are great companies like iTeach (www.i-teach.org.uk) which can provide outstanding support at every juncture of your journey and will also look after your procurement of apps, security and device management at scale. My technician is Martyn Hancock who has been invaluable in the schools I have worked in and with. I have asked Martyn to contribute to the final chapter of this book so that you have expert guidance on the dos and don'ts when setting up security systems in your classroom.

Safeguarding

There are many controls and restrictions that can be applied to an iOS device and they will differ slightly depending on whether you have an iPod, iPhone or iPad. Fundamentally, they all offer control over what can be done with the device.

Here we will look mainly at 'on device' restrictions. There are other methods of securing devices which allow for more automation and remote management (e.g. profiles and mobile device management) and I will touch on these later.

There has been a lot of press recently about children generating huge bills for in-app-purchases (IAP). This can be avoided by turning on a setting in **Restrictions** and parents not giving children their iTunes password (which has a related credit/debit card).

To access the restrictions go into **Settings – General – Restrictions**. From here you can **Enable Restrictions** and will be prompted to set a passcode.

This can be different to the overall device passcode or the same, it's up to you. Don't forget this passcode or you will have to reset the iPad to remove the restrictions. Enter the passcode twice to confirm it. You can now begin setting your restrictions.

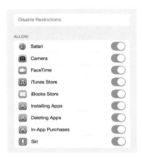

The top half of the restrictions are sliders and they are largely self-explanatory.

For example:

● If you want to remove web-browsing capability from your device then you would disable Safari and make sure that no third-party web browsers are installed.

● Disabling the camera also disables FaceTime.

● The iTunes Store is only for music, film and TV rentals and purchases. This can be disabled from here.

● You can prevent apps being installed by using the Installing Apps slider.

● You can prevent apps being deleted by using the Deleting Apps slider.

● The in-app-purchases slider disables and prevents the IAP mechanism from working, thereby preventing the problem alluded to above.

● Disabling Siri is dependent on the device having Siri (which is a voice recognition system).

The next section of restrictions are all about what type of content you wish to allow or disallow.

1. You can specify the region you are in so that the ratings are appropriate for you.

2. You can turn off any explicit music, music videos or podcasts from the iTunes store.

3. You can specify what age-range films are allowed (these only apply to content purchased through the iTunes store).

4. You can specify whether to allow TV programmes to be purchased through the iTunes store.

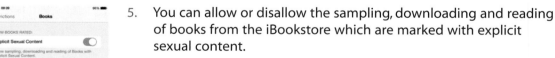

5. You can allow or disallow the sampling, downloading and reading of books from the iBookstore which are marked with explicit sexual content.

6. In the Apps Restrictions section, you can allow or disallow apps based on their App Store age ratings, which are submitted and approved by Apple. Be careful with this setting as it may prevent the installation of seemingly harmless apps. This is usually because the app allows access to the internet and it could therefore theoretically allow age 17+ content through.

7. The Siri restrictions allow you to prevent Siri from recognising explicit language and from performing web searches using Wikipedia, Bing and Twitter.

8. The web content filtering setting enables you to allow all websites, to limit adult content or to limit web usage to only specific websites (in the form of a whitelist). With Limit Adult Content enabled, the iPad tries to prevent access to adult content. There is a caveat with this setting, however: I can find no documentation on Apple's website which explains how or by what mechanism this setting filters web searches. This setting can block totally innocuous educational websites so use with caution.

When you limit access to Specific Websites Only, you have to specify what sites you wish to allow. A pre-filled list suggests about ten known safe sites but you can erase these if you wish and add your own whitelist. This is particularly useful for very young children and also when the device is being used in an online exam.

9. The Require Password setting allows you to either require the Apple ID password for purchases (free or paid) immediately and for each subsequent download or only once every 15 minutes. For example, if the 15 minute setting was enabled you could download an app after entering the Apple ID password and for the next 15 minutes you could download apps without being prompted for the Apple ID password.

The next section of restrictions enable you to allow or disallow, in a very granular fashion, access to all the privacy settings.

You can specify whether you wish to allow the user to turn on or off location services either globally or per app (GPS location services are used to determine your approximate location and they are used in many apps, the best example of which would be weather apps where your local weather is shown).

You can define settings with the same level of granular control for access to your contacts, calendar, reminders, photos (Camera Roll), Bluetooth sharing, built-in microphone, Twitter account (which you can sign in to globally on the iPad), Facebook account (again, you can sign in to this globally).

The final section determines whether you want the device user to be able to make changes to Accounts.

This setting prevents the user adding or deleting accounts in Settings (mail contacts and calendars, Twitter, Facebook).

You can also allow or disallow the user setting a Volume Limit.

The Game Centre controls prevent the user from partaking in Multiplayer Games and from Adding Friends, but these settings do not remove the Game Centre app.

There is one more extremely useful setting for restricting the device but it resides in another menu. This feature is called Guided Access. You can get to it from **Settings – General – Accessibility**.

From this menu you can specify what types of accessibility features you wish to enable. These settings can assist users who have vision, hearing and motor problems.

The feature we want to look at is under the Learning subheading called Guided Access. When you enter this menu you can turn on Guided Access and set a passcode.

Guided Access allows you to lock a user into an app, disable or enable certain areas of the screen, enable or disable the physical buttons on the iPad and prevent the device from rotating when it is turned.

To turn this feature on, firstly turn on the Accessibility Shortcut slider, then you need to triple-click the home button on the iPad when you are in the app you wish to 'lock'. This will bring up the Guided Access screen where you can specify your options, switch off rotation and make certain areas of the screen 'dead' by drawing on the display.

To end Guided Access, triple-click the home button, enter your passcode and tap **End**.

As you can see, there are a lot of restrictions that you can enable on each device according to your needs and requirements, but this is a manual process for each device. If you only have a very small number of devices then this manual process is straightforward to administer, but when the number of devices grows then so does the amount of administration.

Luckily, there are ways that the administration of the restrictions can be automated and streamlined. Here is a brief overview:

Apple Configurator

This is a Mac-only application and is available for free download from the Mac App Store. This application allows you to bulk set-up, configure and deploy iOS devices. It can handle mass updating of the iOS version, restoring a master 'image' of one iOS device (and its configuration profiles) onto many devices.

A configuration profile is a series of settings wrapped up in one file. Contained within this profile are a huge number of configurable options, such as device restrictions, wireless network configurations, email accounts, calendar accounts, proxy servers, air printers and Apple TV destinations.

Profiles can be deployed in a number of ways, including emailing them, placing them for download on a web server, installing them through Apple Configurator and through a mobile device management server (MDM).

MDM

This is the biggie – it is the mechanism that makes remotely managing iOS devices possible. An MDM server allows you to enrol your devices and then manage them wirelessly. You can remotely set configuration changes, deploy apps, wipe devices, locate devices and remove forgotten passcodes, and that is only scratching the surface. There are a myriad of MDM providers out there, some of which are free and some are paid for. A great free MDM is Meraki, which you can sign up for at www.meraki.com. They also make amazing network equipment, switches and wireless access points.

I could write a whole lot more on Apple Configurator, MDM solutions and large-scale deployments, but it is enough to know about them for now. When your confidence increases, along with the need to manage more devices, this will lead you to find out more.

To sum up: deploying iOS devices on any scale is getting much easier thanks to new tools from Apple and third parties, and I can't see this trend changing.

Social media and e-safety

At this point, I think it is important to mention social media and, in particular, Twitter. Without a doubt, Twitter has had the biggest influence on my personal CPD throughout my career and I have made true friends, met top colleagues, shared resources, learned a huge amount from other people and have been able to effectively communicate with parents, community members and other schools.

If you haven't used Twitter before, I recommend that you open a personal account and have a play around with its many functions. You are only allowed to use a maximum of 140 characters to send a message so it is a great summarising tool. Once you have created your account, I suggest you follow the top ten educators I have listed below so that you can start to build up an effective network of support from highly respected practitioners and leaders who will be happy to help you on your personal and school's digital journey.

Mark Anderson – @ICTEvangelist
Sheli Blackburn – @SheliBB
Martin Burrett – @ICTmagic
Dan Edwards – @syded06
Gavin Smart – @gavinsmart
Fraser Spiers – @fraserspiers
Steve Wheeler – @timbuckteeth
Joe Dale – @joedale
iPadupdate – @ipadupdate
Matthew Pullen – @mat6453

On the subject of social media, however, it is worth thinking about creating a social media charter with your pupils. Thanks to a close friend of mine, Henry Platten, who runs a company called eTreble9, specialising in e-safety in schools, I have provided you with his top ten tips to get you started.

10 top tips to get your school started in e-safety

- **Protect your school's online identity:** register your school name on the key social media sites to ensure no one else can set up an account in your name.

- **Empower pupils:** give them the skills and support to help other pupils stay safe.

- **Create an e-Safety group:** the head, a governor and pupil governor/student council member should all be part.

- **Obtain parental consent:** ensure you have signed consent from parents to be able to use photos of pupils on social media.

- **Create a school code of conduct:** involve the pupils, staff and parents in designing your own bespoke code of online conduct.

- **Check device restrictions:** as well as firewalls protecting and blocking content you should also ensure the filter restrictions for different devices, to help keep pupils safe – especially if they use devices on other Wi-Fi networks.

- **Monitor any mentions about the school:** set up email alerts so you can identify any time the school name is used online (e.g. Google alerts).

- **Provide briefings for new NQTs, staff and parents:** when new members join your school community it is important they know how to stay safe and about the school's code of conduct.

- **Staff appropriate use:** they should not be friends online with pupils or parents.

- **Check your followers:** make sure you're connected to appropriate accounts.

Source: eTreble9 www.eTereble9.com

You will quickly see the benefit of social media to your own CPD and will find ways in which sites like Twitter can enhance teaching and learning opportunities in your classroom. However, one step at a time – the benefits of social media in education is a book for another day.

Here is a screenshot of my personal Twitter account for you to use Aurasma and see what it looks like in action.

So, you are now at a point where you need to pause and reflect a little on your digital journey as a school leader. There are five key pillars you will need to consider: vision, infrastructure, identifying leaders, deployment and technical support. I have listed these in the 'ideal world' model below. Okay, here goes!

Ideal world model

1. Vision

How exactly do you see the technology enhancement at your school changing the teaching and learning policy? What do you want it to achieve?

Start small: think about a focus group of pupils to evaluate, a key strand of a core subject or empower a group of teachers to assess impact.

Have a clear vision, aims to evaluate against and communicate this effectively to children, teachers, parents and community members.

2. Infrastructure

Without infrastructure your vision is dead and you risk losing your supporters pretty quickly.

Ideal world:

- Your bandwidth would be huge – the bigger the better
- You would have a robust wireless system throughout the school which allows multiple devices to function effectively.

You have decided on a cloud solution for storing content (e.g. Google Drive) and have found out if this is possible on your infrastructure model.

Communicate this to all key stakeholders!

3. Identifying leaders

You must create your digital team.

Ideal world:

This will consist of you as the head teacher and:

- E-learning manager
- Lead teaching assistant

● Pupil digital leaders.

This team will ensure that you have distributed leadership at all levels in your school.

Together, your digital team will drive forward the school vision with passion.

4. Deployment

Deployment depends on vision, infrastructure and identifying leaders but you do have choices. For example:

● All teachers to have iPads first

● A set of iPads to be shared across school

● One-to-one iPads across a key stage

● A department set

● One-to-one provision across whole school.

There is no *ideal world* here, as it all depends on your vision, budget, expertise at the journey start and what you are trying to achieve.

5. Technical support

You will need technical support from your local authority, an outside company or your own technician to:

Ideal world:

- Update and install apps
- Deal with security settings
- Turn ideas into action
- Deliver staff training and support.

This role should complement that of the e-learning manager and should ensure that the magic can happen in your school!

If you are a head teacher, I recommend that you use these five pillars to inform a two-year implementation plan in your school. Take small steps to empower your digital team, invest in a solid infrastructure and secure budgets and technical support, building it around the vision that you and your team have agreed on.

If you are a teacher, you probably have a huge smile on your face at the moment as you now realise that you don't have to be a technology genius to use iPads in your lessons. Quite the opposite – you should be concentrating on how you are going to change the way you deliver your message to the pupils, how you will improve your practice, how you are determined to evolve and match the needs of the 21st century learner and how determined you are to be a learner with your pupils on this digital journey. So, what are your small steps?

Mark Anderson has formulated a maturity model for teachers about to embark on this exciting journey.

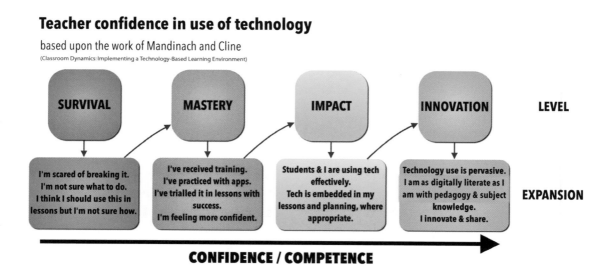

Teacher confidence in use of technology

based upon the work of Mandinach and Cline

(Classroom Dynamics: Implementing a Technology-Based Learning Environment)

SURVIVAL — **MASTERY** — **IMPACT** — **INNOVATION** — **LEVEL**

I'm scared of breaking it. I'm not sure what to do. I think I should use this in lessons but I'm not sure how.

I've received training. I've practiced with apps. I've trialled it in lessons with success. I'm feeling more confident.

Students & I are using tech effectively. Tech is embedded in my lessons and planning, where appropriate.

Technology use is pervasive. I am as digitally literate as I am with pedagogy & subject knowledge. I innovate & share.

EXPANSION

CONFIDENCE / COMPETENCE

Source: Mark Anderson, Teacher Confidence in Using Technology, *ICTEvangelist* (8 September 2013). Available at: http://ictevangelist.com/teacher-confidence-using-technology/. Based on the work of Ellen Beth Mandinach and Hugh F. Cline, *Classroom Dynamics: Implementing a Technology-Based Learning Environment* (Hillsdale, NJ: Lawrence Erlbaum, 1994).

But before you start charging back through your classroom door and implementing all your fabulous new digital ideas, take a look at this brief checklist. It's important!

● Has your school's technology vision been clearly communicated to you?

● Have your eyes been opened to all the exciting possibilities that you and your co-pilot learners are about to embark on?

● Do you have a clear project or curriculum area you are going to focus on to start with?

Chapter 8

Some frequently asked questions

So, here we are. We have arrived at the last chapter of *Freaked Out* – but remember that this is just the start of your wonderful journey.

Via the @Freaked_Out123 Twitter channel, I have been engaging with followers and holding a weekly digital forum where, as a group, we have built a community to share good practice and resources. Here are ten commonly asked questions that followers wanted answers to:

Q. Is there a correct balance between digital and nature? (Craig Armiger)

When looking at this from a school's perspective it has to be all about balance. The school's nature reserve, eco club and development of the outdoor environment is just as essential as a clear understanding of the role that technology can play in learning. However, I believe that if enough imagination and creativity go into it, then both nature and technology together can be a magical combination. Think about weather stations in schools, Wi-Fi enabled woodlands where you can scan QR codes which give you information about a particular plant, or cameras which capture birds nesting and hatching, flowers opening and aquatic animals going about their daily business. These amazing tools were not available to us a decade ago, so it has to be a good thing for our young curious minds to explore the wonderful opportunities that nature affords us.

When out on a bike ride, I enjoy stopping for a moment with my iPhone camera to capture the sun glistening off a pond or a wonderful beach horizon. This does not stop me from appreciating the simplicity and beauty of my surroundings. It allows me to catch a moment and share the joy of that experience later with family and friends.

Q. What are main stumbling blocks that hinder schools' development on their digital journeys? (Emma Howell-Protheroe)

I could probably write a book on this question alone. However, to break it down into small parts, I think the main stumbling blocks usually are (in no particular order):

- The head teacher struggles with having the vision.
- Lack of Wi-Fi within the school (and in most cases within the local authority).
- Teachers who are unwilling to change their practice to fit the needs of the 21st century learner.

These seem to be the main problems I have encountered while working with schools and local authorities. I firmly believe that for the journey to be a successful one, you must have a vision which you stick to and communicate clearly to all stakeholders, you must work extremely hard and not be afraid to make mistakes and learn from them, and you must involve your digital leaders from day one.

Q. How can schools rise to the challenge of keeping up with the pace of innovation in the digital world? (Catherine Place)

In short, I don't think schools can. The secret is to ensure that the infrastructure within your school is sufficiently robust so that as technology and priorities change, whatever devices or equipment are placed on that infrastructure they are going to work. I feel that if schools can stay two or three years behind the latest digital technological innovations in the big wide world then they are doing very well. However, it isn't always about having the latest innovations. I believe it's about creatively using the technologies you currently have, giving pupils the freedom to express themselves with existing technologies and making sure that the school has a clear vision and action plan over a three-year cycle. It isn't about ICT investment any more; it's about technology to improve teaching and learning experiences, which surely must be a priority for all schools.

Q. What are the main challenges that face comprehensive teachers compared to primary where time is more flexible? (Damian Benney)

I don't think that this is a time issue; I think it's more of a cultural issue. For far too long, in my opinion, many comprehensive teachers, having isolated themselves within departments and within classrooms, feel that they 'own' that part of the curriculum or the school's learning journey. We should open this up and give opportunities, for example, to the modern foreign languages department to work closely with the English department. Linking technology across these two departments would be absolutely mind-blowing – for instance, with apps like the

Moving Tales series you can translate wonderful stories into Spanish and French at the touch of a button, which would help to develop creative writing across both subjects.

The current curriculum and education system from pupils aged 11–14 and beyond is the reason, I believe, that the majority of comprehensive schools still teach to GCSE outcomes. Surely, the job of schools and educators is to inspire, engage and enthuse. Several comprehensive schools I have worked with have managed to do this – they are using technology brilliantly and also get outstanding GCSE results. It comes down to the leadership of the school: vision and curriculum planning are critical and a willingness to be innovative and creative is essential.

Q. With a small budget where do you start? (Fiona Thomas)

With a small budget you start small and work with a group of pupils and a lead teacher who is able to prove that the vision actually works. We did exactly this at the last school at which I was head. We spent six to eight months working with a group of eight pupils and eight iPads to craft our programme carefully. It is so important at the start to be able to prove that you can raise attainment, self-esteem and aspirations by using technology, having a creative curriculum and exercising great pedagogy.

Q. Will using ICT to write diminish children's skills when they go back to writing with a pen? (Ian Trimbell)

I see using a keyboard (or stylus) and handwriting as two distinct skills. We have to teach children how to write; it's a skill they are always going to need. However, being controversial, I would also question the importance of it in today's society and job market. Nevertheless, because our education system insists in placing huge importance on it, we often teach children how to master writing to such a degree that other skills are neglected. The secret is balance and a combination of teaching children how to use a stylus on devices and to type effectively and also to be able to write well using a pen or pencil at a younger age. This will arm our pupils with a distinct set of skills that every child should have the opportunity to possess.

Q. Is there always an app for something? (Dan Edwards)

I often discuss this question at length. In our roles, technician Martyn Hancock and I both get asked to name a good maths or history app. There probably are good subject apps out there but I certainly wouldn't recommend any of them. This journey is all about excellent teachers using technology effectively. Boring stuff on an iPad is still boring stuff. Don't look for the quick fix or the app that can solve all your problems – they don't exist. A skilled practitioner should think creatively about engaging pupils and delivering excellent teaching and learning. Some of the most effective apps on your iPad are the most simple ones: the video/camera, the timer, the speaker and the calendar. All of these tools have the potential to transform your classroom.

Q. How do you print from an iPad? (Rebecca Williams)

You should aim to limit printing from digital devices as you should be looking for ways to save your learning electronically. However, there will be certain pieces of digital learning that you will want to print. To do this you will need an AirPrint compatible printer, of which there are hundreds, connected to the same network as the iPad. The alternative is to convert an existing printer by connecting it to a computer on the same network as your iPads and using software which enables AirPlay functionality. Examples of this software include Printopia and HandyPrint.

Q. What case can I get for my school's iPads? (Anon.)

This is almost an impossible question to answer. It depends on many factors, such as the age of the end users, the environment in which the device is going to be used and budget. I would suggest contacting schools or professionals directly or through Twitter who are running similar programmes to ask them what they are using and what are the pros and cons. I would also recommend visiting technology shops and examining different cases before procuring on a large scale. Unfortunately, price is not a clear indicator of quality when it comes to iPad cases.

Q. How do I take a screenshot? (Anon.)

To take a screenshot press the home button and the power button at the same time. The image will then be saved in your Camera Roll.

 I truly hope you are no longer freaked out! It has been an absolute pleasure to give you the key ingredients I have found to be successful over the last few years. Good luck on your journey and remember, as Malcolm X once said, 'Education is our passport to the future, for tomorrow belongs to the people who prepare for it today.'

If you would like to get in touch or attend a course, please contact me.

Simon Pridham @Freaked_Out123

A useful glossary

3G (third generation) – access technology that is widely commercially available for connecting mobile phones and tablet devices.

4G (fourth generation) – as above but at a much faster pace.

8mm HD – an application which allows you to create old 8mm movies in real time.

AirPlay – the ability to mirror the content on your tablet device or phone to another location such as a whiteboard.

AirPrint Compatible Printer – printers that are compatible with Apple's AirPrint software for wireless printing from the iOS.

App – a computer program designed to run on smartphones, tablet computers and other mobile devices.

Android device – an operating system for mobile devices.

Apple TV – a digital media player developed and sold by Apple.

Audioboo – a website and application which allows users to post and share sound files.

Augmented reality – an augmented version of reality which is created by mixing technology with the known world.

Aurasma – an augmented reality application.

Bandwidth – describes the maximum data transfer rate of a network or internet connection.

Bing – a web search engine from Microsoft.

BlackBerry – a line of wireless hand held devices and services.

Blogs – basically, online diaries of information which can be accessed through the World Wide Web. Most of the world's leading digital educators have blogs and are only too willing to share their work, resources, tips and material.

Bluetooth – a wireless technology standard for exchanging data over short distances.

Camera Roll – where the photographs and films taken on your Apple device are stored.

Dropbox – a file hosting service which is cloud based.

e-book – an electronic version of a printed book.

FaceTime – a video chat application developed by Apple which allows you to make video calls over Wi-Fi, 3G or 4G from your device.

Foursquare – a location based social networking website for mobile devices.

Google – a web search engine that lets you find other sites on the web based on keyword searches. Google the company also provides other services such as Goggle Apps and Google Apps for Education.

Google Drive – a cloud storage service that allows you to store documents, photos, videos and more online.

iBookstore – Apple's platform for selling e-books.

iCloud – Apple's cloud storage and cloud computing service from Apple.

iMovie – a movie making application for Apple's iOS operating system.

in-app-purchases (IAP) – purchases made from within a mobile application.

iOS – Apple's operating system.

iPhone – a line of smartphones designed and marketed by Apple.

iPod – a line of portable media players designed and marketed by Apple.

iSight – the name Apple uses for the rear - facing cameras on the iPad, iPhone and iPod touch.

iTunes – a media management software created by Apple for both the Mac and Windows operating systems.

Mobile device management server (MDM) e.g. Meraki – system which allows you to inventory and monitor your mobile devices all in one spot.

Multiplayer Games – a game played by several players.

Podcast – a digital recording of music, news or other media that can be downloaded from the internet to a portable media player.

QR (quick response) code – a machine readable code consisting of an array of black and white squares for storing URLs or other information which can then be read through an app on your phone or device.

Red Laser – a QR code reader and creator application.

Safari – web browser developed by Apple.

screencasting – a digital recording that captures audio, video and pictures and allows you to share them.

Scroll 'n Roll – a text marquee application which allows you to design messages.

Showbie – a free application which can be used to create and collect assignments from the iPad.

Siri – a personal assistant that resides on an iPhone 4S or newer model. It responds to the words you speak rather than requests you type through Apple's iOS operating system.

Sky Drive – Microsoft cloud based application service which allows you to backup, sync and save your files to the cloud.

Skype – a premium voice over service and instant messaging client.

Slider – most commonly used to unlock your iPad so that it becomes functional.

Social media – refers to the means of inter-action among people in which they create, share and/or exchange information in virtual communities. Examples are Facebook and Twitter.

Stylus – a writing instrument used to enter information or write on a touch screen.

Symbaloo – a visual bookmarking tool which acts as a personal start page that allows you to navigate the web.

Twitter – an online social media and microblogging service.

URL – (uniform resource locator) also known as a web address.

Wi-Fi – a wireless networking technology that allows computers and other devices to com-municate over a wireless signal.

WordPress – free and open source blogging tool.

YouTube – an online video sharing website which can be accessed by any member of the general public.

iTeach

Some accompanying screencasts in this book were kindly produced by iTeach (http://www.i-teach.org.uk). iTeach is Wales' leading company in providing a dedicated consultancy, training and installation service for Apple technology in business and education.

iTeach was established in 2012 to help educational establishments and businesses manage the transition from a traditional ICT suite to a post PC era.

About the author

 **Simon Pridham** has successfully managed and implemented a mobile device learning programme as head teacher of Casllwchwr Primary, which is frequently named as one of the UK's leading schools in using technology. Simon has been Lifelong Intergenerational Furthering Education (LIFE) Programme Manager across Wales and has also worked closely with the country's Education Ministers as a member of the Welsh Government Practitioners Panel and the National Digital Learning Council.

He is co-founder and Director of Aspire 2Be (www.aspire2b.eu) who are a leading Ed Tech company working with schools, local authorities and governments in rolling out technology-led programmes. For further information on Simon or Aspire 2Be please contact simon@aspire2b.eu, @freaked_out123 or visit www.aspire2b.eu.